# Paw Talk

# Paw Talk

## Lessons on Living from Man's Best Friend

*Stephen Mathis*

Writers Club Press
San Jose New York Lincoln Shanghai

**Paw Talk**
Lessons on Living From Man's Best Friend

Writers Club Press
an imprint of iUniverse.com, Inc.

For information address:
iUniverse.com, Inc.
620 North 48th Street, Suite 201
Lincoln, NE  68504-3467
www.iuniverse.com

ISBN: 0-595-01067-9

Printed in the United States of America

# PREFACE

In our dreams we experience fanciful notions. Kaleidoscopic images shift like waves in our subconscious mind as we slumber—creating endless varieties of messages with information. Sometimes we are aroused by the reality of our dreams and we awaken to seek the safety of our consciousness, or we awaken to make note of a brilliant idea. Sometimes we recall these images and most of the time we let them sleep. It was in such a heightened state of mind that I imagined what it would be like having a conversation with my dog, "Buster." He spoke to me. In the dream he was helping me to understand the deeper meanings of the daily dramas I experience as I endeavor to deal with life's little circumstances. He let me get outside of myself and see things differently, from his perspective. He was not judgmental—just sincere and truthful. Seeing my world through his eyes made me wonder what insights about ourselves we would gain if our pets could only talk! Perhaps they could offer some lessons for living the best possible life and coping with life's ups and downs.

"Most dogs don't think they're human; they know they are"

Jane Swan

"Man bites dog!" is news. "Dog teaches man about family values!" is not. It's pet justice. What does a dog know about family values? A doggoned lot! Family values are actions, feelings, core beliefs and rules of conduct that are important to all members of a family, because everyone shares the same needs and these values benefit everyone in the group. They also benefit every individual of the group. A family can best be described as a group under one authority. In dog language, this authority is known as our "Master" or "Mistress." Well, everyone in the same family has wants and needs in common with other members of the group. And because all of us, dogs and people, have lots of different wants and needs, there are as many varieties of "families" as there are different breeds of dogs! Some of us can belong to several families. For example, a work group, a household group, a social group, a club group like the canine club, and so forth. Families can also be very small, with only two members, or very, very large that could include all dogs and people in the world!

Affectionately known as "man's best friend," I'm an old dog that has learned a lot about people and human relations. I've been in the relationship business all of my life! I know what I'm barking about! Dogs develop extraordinary people skills and the ability to bond with people. Judging from the people I've observed—they could use our help. Good relationships between people and their pets develop as we discover needs that we have in common. We pets share a need to be loved, appreciated, recognized, praised, and included as part of man's family. We share a need to have shelter and a purpose in life. We share the need to care for someone who cares about us. We share a need to be included, missed, and made to feel useful and important. Sound familiar? What we have in common with man is more important that our differences with mankind. And that's why I'm telling this story. To put it simply, this old dog believes that he can teach people a few new tricks about how to enjoy better relationships with people.

I've observed human behavior for over 80 dog years—that's approximately 15 homosapien years. Getting these things that we both need is conditioned on our ability to develop a mutual positive attitude of love, trust, patience,

"When I carefully consider the curious habits of dogs I am compelled to conclude that man is the superior animal. When I consider the curious habits of man I confess, my friend, I am puzzled."


Ezra Pound

intimacy, forgiveness, loyalty, and respect. These are words of endearment, and familiarity that family members demonstrate toward one another. And they are interrelated. Getting what you want and then enjoying it is the secret of a happy dog's life.

An elder canine, I'm old enough to be philosophical about life and what's important—and what's not important! I'm a survivor because I've learned how a non-resistant attitude will overcome almost any adversity. I've discovered that the secret of my life is my attitude! Some very smart dogs do some dumb things, while ordinary dogs like me with only average IQ's live our lives quite successfully. That's because we learn to adapt to man's world. Our instincts and intuition are natural attributes that we pets possess. We are born with these gifts. Our native practical intelligence helps us to understand and respond to life's events and we learn to trust these natural instincts and abilities. We pets learn to be masters of non-verbal communication. We learn to connect and communicate by using body language and developing good skills of observation. We listen with our whole body. We dogs sit up straight, nod, maintain good eye contact, and sometimes bark our approval or disapproval. We learn that sometimes saying nothing is better than saying just anything! We learn how silence is a useful device to communicate. All of our learning, you see, is through our five senses of sight, smell, touch, taste, and hearing. And even though we can't talk your language, we have learned to accept this adversity of life and not see it as a limitation.

Recently a young man named David died at the young age of thirty-four. He was a lover of dogs and had two dogs of his own. He died of AIDS. AIDS is a terrible disease. Dogs don't get AIDS, but people do! What happens to his dog now? It's sad when a pet outlives his best friend and owner, because nobody cares quite as much about you as your first soul mate. The object of your love and dependence is suddenly gone forever!

Losing someone you love is like being out of a job. It creates a void. Things are never the same. Death changes everything! You grieve. It made me feel

"The only human quality he lacks is that of speech."

Alfred Brehm

sad that he was such a young man, and it only reminded me of life's frailty. Life is short! It makes me appreciate the present moment, and realize how precious we are for one another. As man's best friend, companion, soul mate, ally, and helpmate, I've got my own opinions based on years of people watching. I want to share some experiences that exemplify these family ties we have in common.

Over the years, I've heard a lot of dog tales about man's inhumane treatment of animals. I've heard how pets are used by hospitals for medical experiments. And I've heard reports about the large number of pets who are abandoned or abused by people. But, I've also observed man's inhumanity to man. Man is a breed addicted to discrimination in every form, and anything different is also suspicious to mankind. One way we can be sure that our differences do not cause trouble is to respect our differences and honor the diversity of each others' characteristics, habits, and beliefs. Then we can live in peace and harmony and appreciate our differences.

When I was only a few weeks young, I was sent to a pet store for adoption. My mother stayed behind. My brothers and sisters were also sent away. Mom told us not to be too concerned about our futures because we all had good genes and we'd find good homes. An orphan, I arrived at the pet store and found myself placed in a small cage facing the store entrance. I had a great view of the room. I could watch the customers who entered the door and see other puppies and pets. I had never seen such a variety of us. Some people seemed to know exactly what they had come for, and asked for a pet by its name. That's when I learned we all had different names. I was called a "pug" dog. I didn't look like the others, so I thought "pugs" must be special. I got plenty of attention. Although, some of the other puppies seemed to be more popular with customers! Some kids had never seen my kind, and thought I was "ET" or someone famous like that! Others remarked how "cute" I was. They liked my wrinkled, flat nose, soft floppy ears and curled tail! Some customers confused me with a "Boxer"—another breed of small dog. And, I overheard that I had cousins and was related to some other breeds like the "Pekinese" and "Chow" dogs. And that's how I heard that I

"A dog has the soul of a philosopher"

Plato

was Asian American. We all had different origins and that impressed me. Since that time I've met other pugs—some that are fawn color like me, and others who are black. I've seen dogs with black tongues; brown eyes, blue eyes, and we come in all sizes. There are dogs with curled tails, like mine, and dogs with short tails, long tails, and no tails! There are mongrels of unknown ancestry and pedigree dogs with illustrious lineage. There are "toy" dogs and "miniature" dogs too! And dogs, like people, are international. We all have interesting and different origins. There's the Japanese Chin dog, the German Shepherd, French Bulldog, Finnish Spits, English Cocker Spaniel, Norwegian Lundehund, Italian Greyhound, Irish Sitter, Belgian Sheepdog, English Bulldog, Chinese Pug (that's me!), and many, many more!

As the door opened and a bell sounded to let the storekeeper know that a customer had entered, a young guy walks into the store and heads toward my cage. I could tell that he was on a mission. He pointed in my direction and the next thing I knew, I was placed on the floor as the guy knelt down to get a closer look at me and pat me on the head. I was relieved to get a stretch and decided to wander around. I had a good feeling about this guy, and decided to sniff him out! This was a good move and the guy reached out to hold me. I wiggled my tail to signal my approval. He picked me up in his arms and my future flashed before me—I had found my new owner! On the spot, he told the sales clerk that he wanted me and would take me home. "How much?", he asked. "No problem," he said. He paid the man, signed some adoption papers, and continued to hold me while he did some more shopping for a bed, water bowl, dish, collar and leash, a soft toy, puppy food and other personal care items he knew I would need. And that's when it hit me—this guy chose me. I didn't choose him. Love is like that. It's bestowed. Isn't God's love for man a lot like an owner's love for his pet? It's not earned. When we left the store I felt sorry for my little friend, a girl pug who had been in the cage next to mine. She had been whimpering and crying for her mother. I had tried to cheer her and offer some comfort. I glanced back at her to signal that everything will work out for her too! I felt happy that I had

"It's not much of a tail, but I'm sort of attached to it"

Eeyore

been chosen. I was filled with hope, excitement, and anticipation about my future. I also wished her a positive thought.

A place called "home" was a strange, new and wonderful house with a yard. It wasn't at all like the kennel at the farm where I was born. For one thing, there were no other dogs around. It was all mine! Two aspects of body language that are of special interest to dogs and other animals are "territory" and "positioning." I could hardly wait to explore my new surroundings and mark my territory. I was excited and nervous. I had to whittle. That's when I was introduced to paper training—newspapers spread out on the floor where I was supposed to do my business. I soon discovered that I could do my business in the yard—and it didn't make as much work for Him. Also, it was more private. I always received praise as a "good dog" when I finished. Like children, pets learn when they are encouraged to learn. I explored the yard—enjoying the scents of fragrant garden flowers; the cool refreshing taste of dew drops on the grass and leafy bushes; and I enjoyed the feel of soft earth beneath by paws. As I grew older, it became my custom to take walks around the neighborhood, and I could scout out new routes and meet other dogs. I got a lot of attention on those walks—especially in the late afternoons and on evening walks. People would come over to look at me and check Him out! He said some of them were "cruising." I'm not sure if the people were really curious about me, or if they saw me as an excuse to meet Him. Anyway, we both seemed to be getting something from our walks!

My bed was a large wicker basket with a pillow. It was placed in the bedroom next to His bed. As I got older I developed a habit known as "snoring." Sometimes I was so loud that I woke myself up! My bed was moved into the garage, which was OK too because this is Southern California. It's never too cold outdoors for a dog—well, almost never. In colder climates my dog pals have doghouses. I had my own pet door to enter and exit the house as I pleased. Things were good. Then I had my first family crisis. It was about boundaries. I was not allowed on household furniture and was scolded for climbing on the furniture. My repeated attempts to help myself to a couch or soft chair were not appreciated and the experience taught me an important lesson. This little clash of agendas marked a turning point in my development and growth from child to adult. I learned the difference between "Me" and "We." I was part of a family now! I had to think of what makes Him happy as well as thinking of myself. Very soon after I became accustomed to my new home, I was enrolled at a school. This was not an ordinary school, but a private obedience school to learn discipline. They taught me some commands that would help me to communicate with Him. I was taught some tricks and was rewarded with treats for performing them correctly. At my first several classes I learned to "sit," "heel," "come," "go," "stop," and "shake paws." It took a lot of practice, but over time I managed to master these skills. This was also my first important lesson in negotiation. In negotiation you learn to trade favors. In exchange for each successful action there is a reward. A reward quickly reinforces success. Being successful is doing what will endear you to people. Your owner wants you to make him feel proud and important! He wants you to make him feel special. If he knows that he is special to you, then he will keep you around to get that special attention—because you improve the quality of his life. People are easy. They want to know more that you care about them than how much you know! Even the dumbest dogs and laziest of dogs have it made if they understand this important truth. If you give little you will get little in return. It was a big step in my development when I realized that people could help me do a better job than I could do alone. The first time I took a walk around my neighborhood, He put me on a leash. I knew the commands that I had learned. I had been taught to "heel," "stop," "sit." and "go." But my collar was uncomfortable and it really hurt my ego. That was until I met "Killer!" He was a 60 pound Bulldog—all teeth and muscle. He was not on a leash. Faster than the crack of thunder he ran over to my side of the street and tried to provoke a fight. He flashed his teeth and snarled at me. My reflex was to stand my ground and stand still! I was thankful for the collar and leash that saved my tail! He hoisted me upwards and held me high in his arms above the jaws of Killer. Whew! That was a narrow escape. I've also had some close calls with moving traffic—when I have stepped off a street curb and found myself in the direct path of a rubber tire. The collar and leash spared my life on those occasions as well!

One day a visitor came to our house—and stayed. It was totally unexpected. She was a stray kitten who had been abandoned by her mother. Actually I think that her mother had been feeding in the neighbor's garbage and was trapped and sent away. So this wild-eyed little furry creature who was lost and stranded and had found my kibble bowl.

She was helping herself while she meowed and cried for her mother to find her. He heard her cries and gave her some milk. She stayed around the yard and never left. I watched with curiosity, but I didn't object. I was too young to know that cats and dogs were supposed to be enemies. So I began to play with her. I knew she was not a dog, but I couldn't let that interfere with our friendship. Although we were different, we made a good team. We learned to open doors together, warn one another of approaching danger, and kept an eye out for each other. She did some disgusting things sometimes—like dragging home a bird or a mouse that she was proud to have caught. Her intentions were good, but it upset Him too! It was just her way of reminding us whom she was and she was proving her hunting skills as a predator. He had never cared much one way or another about cats, so it surprised me when he made "Kitty" an official member of our family. He bought her a food bowl and a litter box. I guess she was here for the long term. I began to worry that she would get more attention than I would! I noticed that she didn't have to go to obedience school and she certainly did not stay off of the furniture! I developed a plan to protest unfair and privileged treatment. When He was away, I'd sit on the sofa or track some dirt into the house. Those temper outbursts only resulted in getting me a scolding with a roll of newspaper and banishment to the yard. So I began to realize that life wasn't always fair and that people do make allowances for individual differences and diversity of lifestyles, based on our genetics and breeding. Because we can't be what we are not, doesn't mean that we are any less important, unloved, or respected. I learned to accept Kitty and let her be the cat in our family. I didn't try to convert her into a dog. In fact, dogs like to be treated like dogs! It's good for our self-esteem. You see, we are proud of being different from other pets. We're not better; we are just different. That's why I like His special friend, the guy who came to live with us. Because I joined the family first, this guy was a little jealous of me. His friend said that I was spoiled because He didn't treat me like a dog. In time I won His friend's affection too. One of the things I like most about this friend is that he treats me like a dog. Kitty and I have a great relationship too! We have grown old together. She shadows me on my daily walks. She keeps an eye out for me—and that's no small favor especially since I now have only one eye.

It was supposed to be a routine visit to the animal hospital "vet" for my annual medical checkup and vaccination shots. He was away on a vacation in Hawaii, and I had been taken to stay with His sister at her home in Fresno, California. She had a large yard and two dogs of her own. They were great fun. I felt like I was on vacation too! We chased a cat. Imagine that! Me, chasing a cat? I guess I forgot my manners. No disrespect to Kitty, but it was good fun and exercise. Anyway, my eye got a good bang during one of those playful skirmishes. I began to feel some discomfort and liquid kept forming in my eye. I kept wiping it with my paw and on the grass. I had some blurred vision in my right eye, but not pain. Apparently I damaged a tear gland that keeps my eye moist and lubricated. My dry eye had become infected and caused mucous to form on my eye. By rubbing the eye, I only irritated the condition more. Well, I guess it was justice for having chased a cat. I felt a little guilty. I had known better. I had developed good kitty karma and I should not have acted so irresponsibly. I now know that each action has a cost and a reward. I was feeling some guilt and feeling bad about that, but did I really deserve this punishment? My visit to the vet escalated to a crisis, when I overheard the doctor's diagnosis. I became alarmed when I heard them describe my condition as advanced glaucoma of the right eye. They said I'd be partially blind. If I were to be permanently handicapped, I thought, maybe I would be eligible for a handicap tag that allows me special privileges, like some people!

I learned that I might even loose my right eye! Why me? They reached Him in Hawaii on vacation. One of the doctors suggested putting me to sleep, a euphemism for putting me down and sending me off to my final resting

"You think dogs will not be in heaven? I tell you, they will be there long before any of us."

Robert Louis
Stevenson

place. I was having difficulty breathing and was real scared. I was worried that I wouldn't see Him again! Do dogs go to Heaven?, I wondered. What do I have to look forward to? Is this another new adventure in my development? I don't know if we have souls but we dogs do feel emotions and have a strong life force to fight for our survival—just like people. I didn't want to find out the answers to my questions just yet, anyway. Some say that our eyes are windows to the soul, so with one bad eye my soul will have only one window! Sometimes He feels that I have a hidden past or a previous life that I don't begin to really understand. I guess there are world religions and lots of people who believe in reincarnation of the soul and that sometimes the soul is reincarnated in an animal's body. He jokes with me about being an ancient Chinese soul in a dog's body. He jokes that when I'm sitting quietly in contemplation I look like a miniature Sphinx—wise and old beyond my years. Sometimes he sees me moving in slow motion when I am smelling a plant's fragrance and He thinks I'm practicing some ancient Chinese martial arts dance, Thai Chi. He was upset and concerned with my diagnosis. He told them that I had insurance. That made the vets happy. They were now ready to do their magic! He asked them to save my one good eye and that I'd have to live with 50/50 vision. That sounded better than 20/20 vision! I was optimistic. You know, the handicapped learn to compensate by developing their other senses. He was told that if my left eye were watched and medicated regularly, it would function normally because the infection had not spread. The doctors said I should recover nicely. I left the hospital doped up on drugs and painkillers. Ever see a dog on drugs? Drugs are bad news. I had no sense of balance, and felt like sleeping most of the time. I also lost my appetite. But I was glad to be alive and knew things would only get better from here on! I was sore for the next few weeks, and had to wear a plastic cone-shaped collar around my neck to avoid bumping into objects until the stitches from my eye had healed. He returned from Hawaii and took me home. He fed me by hand and held ice cubes for me to lick when I was thirsty. He was there loving and caring for me during the recovery period. In several months I was again feeling fine. Every now and then I bump or walk into something. It was over four years ago and I'm still around to enjoy the world. Having one eye seems almost normal to me now.

In fact, I like my soft toys to have only one eye. I chew off the right button. Some people make fun of the way I look. I'm not self-conscious, but I know a lot of people would not love an one-eyed dog the way He loves me. Most people judge things by their outward appearances, actions and conduct. People judge other people by their outward badges—like the car they drive, where they work, their neighborhood, the home they live in, the clothes they wear. My missing eye is a badge of courage that I wear nobly. Because people respond emotionally before they respond intellectually, I find that I get a lot of empathy. Outward appearance is not just about vanity. It's about survival. If you look healthy; if you are well groomed, poised, and active then you have a better chance of gaining acceptance of others. A confident manner and movement is also a trustworthy protection device. Our appearance says more about us than anything we say.

Do you notice that people sometimes look like their dogs and vice versa? It's a strange phenomenon, but dogs often mirror their owners' moods and dispositions. In fact, people's attitude and disposition is also influenced by the mood of other people surrounding them. That's why it is important to exhibit a positive attitude! A positive attitude is always contagious! Sometimes this is called having a "sunny disposition."

Some people like to dress their dogs to look like them! I've seen dogs in sweaters, dogs wearing caps, and a variety of costumes. He took me to a parade once and dressed me up in a leather outfit. Boy, did I look "macho." Most dogs wear either a dog collar or a harness. Some collars can be pretty fancy—like jewelry! But we need collars or a harness to hang our nametags, and, to attach our leash. My favorite leash is the "flex" leash that stretches and gives me a wide path to explore. Sometimes I've gotten tangled around a tree or got caught in a bush, but I like the freedom of a long leash! When I was younger I wore a "choke" leash until I had been trained to follow certain commands on my walks.

I was standing on our curb noticing the large trees next to the streetlight—trying to decide which one to mark, when suddenly I saw my neighbor's dog, Buddy.

"Heaven goes by favor. If it went by merit, you would stay out and your dog would stay in."

Mark Twain

Buddy, stepped onto the pavement to approach me. A car was speeding down the street and I knew Buddy was in its path. I forced a yelp to warn him, but it was too late. He was knocked under the wheel and lay still. My heart sank, as he lay motionless. The car braked to stop. Buddy's owner was just running and screaming. I could feel his panic and pain. He was scared and shaking. It had all happened so fast that I'm sure Buddy didn't suffer. He knelt beside Buddy and cried. He picked Buddy up and rushed away. I heard a car engine start and I saw Buddy's owner drive off with Buddy, I never saw Buddy again. People still talk about Buddy. I hope that dogs like Buddy go to Heaven! Buddy also had a cat! I think cats have a supernatural instinct and they can see ghosts and spirits! Buddy's cat still takes walks around the neighborhood and follows Buddy's old route! Maybe Buddy's walking right along side! People have a spiritual nature to their personalities. Some people have developed this part of themselves more than other people have. There seems to be two aspects of spirituality for mankind. He has a kind and good side as well as a dangerous, dark side. Did you know that animals have a patron saint? I think he was called Saint Francis of Assisi, and he was from a place in Italy. He cared for animals and blessed them! Although I don't know much about religion, I have been taken to the annual Blessing of the Animals. It is always an event I look forward to because I get to see so many other pets. Some are infirm and appear very ill. It's man's spiritual connection that gives man his energy, ambition, hope, and motivation and distinguishes mankind from God's other creatures.

My first California earthquake was quite a jolt! I was enjoying a deep slumber on my pillow in the garage when suddenly waves of motion rolled the ground beneath me and shook the building on its foundation. Everything rattled and vibrated. I was shocked. What mighty force was attacking? My world was crashing down around me! Then there was a strange calm and quiet that followed. I observed no major damage. A few cracks had appeared in the pavement and chimney; some furniture in the house was toppled, but it could have been much worse! I know that He keeps an earthquake survival kit in His garage—with food, water, medicine, and even pet food for such an emergency! I'm glad that He is prepared for the worst and has also made provision for Kitty and I. Living in Southern California, I'm now used to earthquakes. Natural disasters are unpredictable and unavoidable, wherever you live. There are hurricanes along the coastal waters, wind and tornadoes in the Midwest, floods, and forest fires in the mountains, as well as snow avalanches. Natural disasters not only threaten human life, but also jeopardize and can destroy animal life as well. What I've noticed is when there is a natural crisis of any kind—that people pull together to help one another! It proves to be man's finest attribute.

People organize and come to the rescue and support of others in times of trouble.

It was a typical Wednesday morning. I was home alone. He had left the house for work. I had been left indoors because weather forecasters had predicted rain that day. This was the day the maid came to clean the house each week. I thought she had arrived when I heard the noise. It was a loud crash. A burst of glass shattered. This didn't sound like her typical entrance. The noise came from the back door. I stood up to see what was causing such a racket! A man crawled through the door. I had never seen him before. I kept silent and watched. He moved quickly as he entered the bedroom and started opening drawers and looking for things. I saw him take some things and put them in his pockets. He dropped a ring and stopped to pick it up. I knew that he wasn't welcome here because he broke into our house.

Taking things that belong to others is wrong and shows no respect for their ownership. People take dogs that don't belong to them. A little girl pug dog that lived across the street from us was stolen from her home! I tried to think of a way I could make him go away. I had overheard stories about small dogs like myself being locked up in an oven or clothes dryer by a burglar in order to keep them silent! So, I decided not to yelp and howl and call attention to myself. I was too small to attack the intruder, and there was a good possibility that he had a weapon! I ran to the hallway because I knew that if the alarm beam were turned on, I could trigger the security alarm by crossing the beam's path. It didn't work! The alarm beam had been left off today because He had left both Kitty and me indoors because it was a cold, wet and rainy day. But timing is everything! The housekeeper arrived and I heard her key turning the lock on the front door. The burglar heard it too!

"Dogs have belly buttons, too!"

He escaped fast! It's really too bad that people today have to protect themselves from other people! They put bars on their windows, install security devices in their homes and cars, build walls, erect gates, organize neighborhood watch groups, get "watch dogs," buy pepper spray and mace, and plant "protective" landscaping around their homes. Landscaping is something we dogs know a lot about! You see, certain plants—especially varieties of cactus, succulents, and vines can erect barriers even a dog can't penetrate or jump! If people don't respect themselves, then they won't respect others. Dogs know a lot about respect. Younger dogs are respectful of older dogs. When I meet a new pup on my walks, they roll over in a submissive gesture to signal their respect of my seniority. People's attitudes often differ from canine dogma, and the young do not always show courtesy towards their elders.

Mealtime comes twice a day! Food is one of my favorite things in life. We are what we eat. I'm in the "Zone" and get plenty of protein and a balanced diet of meat protein, carbohydrates, and fat. Dog food has become very fancy. There is vegetarian fare; beef jerkys, milk bone and bone marrow treats; meat loafs and stews; combination of rice and lamb, seafood, beef or chicken canned foods, as well as hard, crunchy dry foods. My favorite dog food is flavored with bacon and turkey. But people seem to like sweets the most! People especially like chocolate! But dogs can't eat chocolate! Chocolate makes us sick and acts like a poison to our system. It sure smells good. People like it! Sometimes we like things that aren't good for us—just like people. I'll never forget the night one of His friends fed me chocolate under the table. I thought this guy was being especially nice! I learned later that this fellow really didn't like dogs and that this was his way of trying to get rid of me! I ate the chocolate because it tasted good! But afterwards I was so sick that I vomited on his shoe! My rapid recovery discouraged that person from ever again trying to trick me into eating something that wasn't good for me. Many people and dogs do things that aren't good for them. Sometimes we call these bad practices "habits." He smokes a pipe. I hate second-hand smoke! Why do people smoke? It's not natural. It's an addiction! Taking any drugs can develop into a bad habit. Some foods have bad drugs in them that can also be harmful if eaten in excess— like the effect that chocolate has on dogs. Coffee and tea contain caffeine and many foods contain sugar! In excess these ingredients can also be harmful! People who love chocolate are called "chocoholics" because they are addicted to chocolate! Too much chocolate gives kids bad complexions or a condition called "acne." If you can't kick a particular habit you can learn to manage it. Some people and some dogs overeat! That can be harmful if it isn't under control. You have to care about yourself first if you want to change a habit. You have to care about yourself first if you want to care about others!

One of my bad habits is snoring! I make a lot of racket and this bothers some people. Because my nose is flat and small, I do have a breathing problem. It causes me to cough, snore and make other strange noises from time to time. Sometimes I also make noise when I pass gas! Those are habits that I can't do much about. As I get older, those sounds get louder and more frequent. His father snores when he sleeps or naps in the house and he's older too! It is just one more characteristic we older dogs have in common with older people.

Both dogs and people have habits that can annoy other dogs and people. But to someone, who loves you, some habits can become characteristics that endear you to them. You also can learn to make these little habits work to your advantage. For example, He has a bad habit of leaving his back door to the house open when he returns home from work—even during the summer when the air conditioning is turned on. He forgets to close the door tightly. Kitty and I rather like the convenience of being able to enter and exit His house at will!

My given name is "Buster." I like my name because it's masculine and easy to recognize when I'm called. People call other people many names—not always by their given family names. Some of these names are affectionate nicknames like "Honey," "Sweetie Pie," "Lover," "Baby," "Peaches," "Hotdog," and "Top Dog." I have nicknames too! He calls me "Buggy," "Mr. B," and "Huggy Buggie." Some nicknames I've heard animals called

"The reason a dog has so many friends is that he wags his tail instead of his tongue."

Anonymous

are uncomplimentary names like "Beast" or "Killer." Names can be hurtful and insulting as well as praiseworthy and kind. I guess it makes people feel superior to another person when they call the other person a name that is disrespectful. Names are important because they create an identity for persons and pets. Names can also be descriptive dog names like, for example, "Frenchy," "Spot," "Fancy," and "Rover." Names are labels to distinguish you from others and give you individuality. Some dogs have the same names as people. In fact, pets are often named after people or other pets that are held in high regard. Giving a name should be like bestowing a title or honor. My name is also on my pet tag, which I wear on my collar. If I should ever get lost, I can be returned to my home because I wore a pet tag and because I'm registered with a license. People also have different licenses and identification papers, like their driver's license and social security cards, their Visa account, or e-mail address. Children, like pets, get lost and sometimes separated from their families. If they know their names, a home address or a phone number they can be returned to their homes. There are stray dogs, who are like street people, and have no permanent home. They wander and survive by their wit, cunning, and luck. Too many people and too many dogs are homeless and without a family or friends! But some of these are lucky because they have found each other.

I can keep a secret better than most people can! Keeping a secret is a real sign of friendship. Dogs don't tell what they know. That's another reason we're man's best friends. A best friend is entrusted with private information and is expected to be confidential with this information so it can't be used to hurt the ones they love. People need secrets and privacy to feel powerful. Secrets can be fanciful hopes, notions, and dreams people are afraid to share because they will be ridiculed, embarrassed, or compromised. He often tells me His secrets and things He doesn't discuss with anyone else— like His dreams and ambitions. He knows I won't laugh or disapprove of Him. Knowing His secrets just lets me know Him better! You learn a lot about people's prejudices too— their likes and dislikes. People keep many of these opinions private because not everyone will agree with them. Sometimes He will talk to me about His most private thoughts and problems, and I can't

"To err is human; to forgive is canine"

Anonymous

help Him much except to be there for Him—to listen and comfort Him. Sometimes I worry about Him because I know when He feels alone and must make some tough decisions without anyone's help.

All families have their rituals and traditions that they customarily repeat together. Some families gather together for their evening meal or attend Sunday church worship together. Others plan annual vacation trips or family outings like picnics. Sometimes they even take their dogs! I've been on some great family vacations—like the trip to Yosemite Park. I had a close encounter with a bear on that trip and also was on the lookout for coyotes, if I didn't want to be their lunchmeat! But travel can be exciting! Once I traveled on a plane in the cargo bay. One of the other passengers, a poodle, got kicked off the plane because her owner had a fight with a flight attendant. The passenger wanted to keep the poodle with her inside the plane on her lap and that was against the airline's rules.

A neighbor dog, Charles, once took an overnight trip with his family that required him to stay in a hotel. Since some hotels have rules that restrict pets staying as guests, his family had to hide him. The only way to get to their hotel room was to enter the hotel lobby and walk past the registration and concierge desks in the hotel lobby to the elevator. In order to disguise the fact that they had a dog in tow, his family transported him in a baby carriage in order not to attract attention from the hotel staff. Well, apparently one hotel guest who was standing at the elevator door and also waiting for the elevator to arrive, curiously gazed into the baby carriage to look at the child. The surprised guest pronounced Charles the ugliest "baby" he had ever seen!

Some rituals are more enjoyable than others are. Both dogs and people have rituals! My daily walks are rituals I look forward to each day. Mealtime is another favorite ritual. I also like my dog treats and Kitty likes her catnip and "Royal Catviar." Most of these rituals are important occasions to be with members of your family and act like family. One of my favorite rituals is going to the pet store to shop for food and supplies. I love wandering through the isles and sniffing the packages of dog food. Also, I always meet

"A dog has one aim in life. To bestow his heart."

a few other canines at the store. Another bonus is that the storekeeper always offers me a reward stick to chew after my visit. A trip to the dog groomer is not as much fun, but necessary. I always feel good and look better when I leave the dog groomer. I don't enjoy the bath or blow dryer. I once heard of a dog that passed on at the dog groomer after his blow dry! Although some dogs love water, I don't swim well and try to stay clear of any tubs, lakes, oceans, and yard hoses. When soap gets into my eyes it usually stings, because most dog shampoos are medicated to treat for fleas. Fleas are little varmints that attach themselves to dogs and cats and make us itch and squirm. They are a nuisance and try to make us miserable. People hate fleas too, and have found many ways to control them. There are flea powders, flea foams, flea dips, flea shampoos, flea bombs, flea collars and flea medicines. He has tried all of these methods and products on me. My fear of water began when He dropped me into a swimming pool to see if I could swim. I almost drown! I discovered that even I could swim, although it was with great effort! I had a hard time keeping my head above the water. I was scared and paddled hard and fast to exit the pool. He saw me struggling, so He pulled me out. I felt this had been a test to see if I could save myself in case of an emergency, so I forgave Him for this indiscretion. But I have to say that it made me mistrustful anytime we came near the water. This has proved to be a good lesson in how you build trust with another family member. They learn your strengths and weaknesses, your likes and dislikes. If they are sensitive and thoughtful they will not make you uncomfortable on purpose. Rituals are personal as well as family activities. He likes to wash his own car. Some people like gardening. When He gardens I get to smell all the fresh cut tree branches and new flowers being planted. Rituals are therapeutic and provide a diversion from routine tasks. They are usually productive activities. Most ceremonies that are rituals include food! I enjoy being around on those occasions! There are birthdays, weddings, anniversaries, dinner parties and all kinds of reasons people get together to eat and celebrate!

Most of these ceremonies are events held to pay respect to someone or to honor them by making them feel special. Each of us is special. Like people,

"He hath a share of man's intelligence, but no share of man's falsehood."

Sir Walter Scott

no two dogs are exactly alike. God created everything special. Our world would not be as interesting if we all looked, sounded, or acted the same. And since everyone is special, we have a lot of ceremonies. There are special dogs too! Lassie was a famous dog who became a popular television celebrity because he demonstrated special qualities of courage, strength and ability. He was so admired that he became a hero and a legend. It's important to have heroes because we can learn from them, and we can try to be more like them. Since we learn from observing the behavior of others, our heroes become "role models." But not all role models are celebrities. And not all role models teach good examples. Bad behavior gives others a bad example. That's why we try to be responsible about our actions and do the right thing. If you're bad and get into trouble, there's an expression that you're "in the dog house." Well, that's too close to home.

Everyone needs a job to feel productive and useful! Dogs are no exception! Dogs have a lot of jobs. There are guard dogs, crime dogs, and dogs to lead the blind. There are hunting dogs and dogs that can pull snow sleds. There are sheep dogs to help shepherds and cattle dogs to help herdsmen. There are dogs that star in TV commercials, and others that perform stunts in movies and on television! We dogs perform many jobs and charitable acts. Like people, we have jobs to do to better serve mankind. However, some of the more important jobs that we do are to star in home videos; keep homes safe; keep a lonely night from being lonely; teach children about responsibility; treat people like celebrities when they come home from a hard days' work; make man live a little longer; lower people's blood pressure; agree with everything; and we teach man the meaning of unconditional love! Doing something for nothing is called "charity." I let Kitty eat out of my kibble bowl. I know there is always more where that came from! Charity is a noble act towards another to share responsibility for another's success or misfortune. Family members should always show charity toward one another!

Jobs give our lives purpose and meaning. Sometimes people loose their jobs and have to find another! It's not always easy! Sometimes we are trained to

"Dog's possess something like a conscience."


Charles Darwin

do one thing and then must learn to do another. Once when He lost His job and was worried about money. He told me a secret. He said that if he wasn't able to get a job soon that He would have to start eating my dog food! I believed Him. I think that He was kidding and just having fun with me. Fortunately for me, that has never happened!

Play is having fun! Everyone needs to have a sense of humor and not take himself too seriously! Every one of us should enjoy what we do! If we enjoy what we are doing we will do it better! Howllelujah! I sleep during most of the day waiting for Him to get home from work so that we can take a walk together. I especially like to rest on the Oriental carpet in our living room. I also like to play tag in the grass or roll over for Him to rub my stomach. Sometimes He lets me sit on His chest and I like that too. I like Him to throw my soft toy around for me to retrieve. I also just like to be close to Him. I sit for hours with my chin resting on His shoe as He watches television or reads. I follow Him around the house when He's home alone. Play energizes us and playing well teaches us how to be good sports. That's important! We need to learn to play fair by following rules. Some people only play to win, because they are trained and taught to think that way. But life is not a game. It must be taken seriously, while we learn how not to take ourselves too seriously! And, although we learn from our successes, failures teach us valuable lessons as well. Failures can teach us how to play better and try harder the next time! How we play is important, although winning feels better! First runner up just means you are First Looser. I know a few dogs that are always entered into contests and dog show competitions! There's a lot of pressure on them to perform their acts with no mistakes. But not every contestant can be a winner! In obedience school I didn't win the ribbon, but was still rewarded for my effort. I did finally win a blue ribbon for being "the most unusual" dog in the pet parade. Celebrate effort, because it demonstrates your commitment to change and self-improvement. When we can learn to play well with others, it creates teamwork. Kitty and I are a team. We are an especially good team since we now both have one eye each. Together we have a pair of eyes! It is an important lesson when we learn that by helping each other we can do a better job together than we could do alone.

"No louder shrieks to pitying heaven are cast, when husbands or lapdogs breathe their last."

Alexander Pope

It's an imperfect world. People can change, but dogs will be dogs! People are who they are and dogs remain what they are—man's best friend! Maybe my revelations will add new meaning to the phrase, "it's a dog's life"—living one day at a time without worrying about the future! Yes, there's a lot to be said for that! Worry doesn't add a single day to your life, but creates negative stress, anger and guilt. It can make you feel discouraged. Living in the moment is what a dog's life is all about! We dogs enjoy life one day at a time. In fact, one of His rituals, is to read out loud each morning from a book that He calls His "devotional." Then He talks to God, who is like His "Master" because he tries to follow God's rules each day. Isn't that like living day by day?

It seems that people are fascinated with knowing how their animals and pets perceive them! I guess that's why the comic strips "Citizen Dog" and "Charlie Brown" are so popular with people. More and more talking animals are featured in books, comic strips, TV shows and motion picture films—because we tell things the way we see them, innocently and truthfully! Honestly! What we dogs do for you people! Oh, by the way, my Boss got a new job so there will be plenty of dog food in my cupboard. See how things can work out if you give yourself a little time and have a lot of faith!

There are a few more "family values" and needs I should describe in this dog's tale. They are words like "respect," "responsibility," and "accountability."

Four years have passed since I began this dog's tale, a canine's primer on family values. Dogs, unlike people, never retire since companionship is our greatest virtue! I'm still at my job. I'm now a pooch past my prime and enjoying my "golden years" of serene seniority. Growing older is another of life's rites of passages we dogs share with mankind, which teaches us important lessons in how our elders should be treated. Animals, like people, want to live out the remainder of their days with respect, honest dignity and

"Buy a pup and your money will buy love unflinching."

Rudyard Kipling

purpose. To love and be loved is man's greatest passion, and it is a dog's only aim in life! But if you don't love yourself and if you aren't good to yourself, then it's hard to express these feelings and attitudes toward others, whether they are dogs or people. How we treat others and ourselves is based on respect!

As we grow older we require more assistance and care and this places some added responsibility on our family members. I find that I now need Him more than ever before, because my body parts wear out with age and I require His help to get some things done that once I could do on my own. I also notice that I can't do the same things that I used to do. We took a walk in the forest at Lake Tahoe and when I stopped by a tree trunk to mark my scent, I had difficulty reaching my leg up in the correct position to whittle. So, I just squatted to pee. He could tell that I was disgusted with myself, but I got over it. It didn't embarrass Him because he understood I was doing the best I could and it was OK. And, sometimes I simply forget something I always thought I knew. My memory begins to play funny tricks, sometimes referred to as having "senior moments." Usually these things come back to me and I remember whatever it was I had forgotten, if it was important.

Growing old with grace is also costly, because in an effort to prolong our quality of life, we need someone to help us take better care of our health. This is a big responsibility. He takes me on frequent trips to the veterinarian and chiropractor. I'm prescribed medicines that ease my aches and pains caused by aging. He makes sure I get regular exercise and a balanced diet. I've even been to an acupuncturist!

I've outlived many of my canine friends. For pets who outlive their owners or become to inconvenient to take care of, there are adoption services and pet organizations with volunteer staff people to feed, walk, bathe, and shower dogs with affection. Sometimes a dog is placed in a new home. Sometimes an old dog will be sent to a sanctuary, which is a lot like a retirement home for old people. These are some of the ways we take responsibility for others, and especially our elders.

Like older people, old dogs eventually die! I've learned the reason we all share this natural fate is because of "sin." What is "sin?" It is the religious word used to describe the consequences of failure because mankind did not meet God's objectives, or live up to God's expectations. In an ancient time, the first man and woman, known as "Adam" and "Eve" failed God's test. The test was not to eat a forbidden fruit in God's Paradise, a perfect place where they lived known as the "Garden of Eden." The story describes how Adam and Eve disobeyed God and ate the fruit anyway. So God held them accountable for their disobedience and punished them by making them feel ashamed of their misbehavior and forced them to leave the Garden of Eden. Ever since that time, mankind has been trying to learn how to become more Godlike so mankind will be worthy to see God again and get back into Paradise, called "Heaven." "Heaven" is mankind's reward for living a good life. I hope there's a reward for good dogs too. We have pet cemeteries just like cemeteries for people, when they die. I'm especially hopeful that God has a Heaven for us too. Did you notice that "GOD" spelled backwards is D-O-G! I wonder if that means we dogs are Godlike? I hope to ask God that question someday. We dogs are also held accountable! It simply means that we are expected to take ownership for our actions and be responsible family members! Like we can't go around chasing every cat on the block or barking at every person who comes over to visit Him, or pee in the house, or do things that makes work or causes problems for other family members. Just like God holds mankind accountable, He holds me accountable to be His best and most loyal friend!

Now that I'm older, I get to sleep more and am more contemplative about all things. I think a lot about Him. Since I had no puppies of my own, I devoted all of my paternal instincts and energy towards Him. Together, we've learned how to practice family values and cope with life's ups and downs. Putting family first is "paw-sitively" the secret of a good life!

"Man is troubled by what might be called the dog wish, a strange and involved compulsion to be as happy and carefree as a dog."

James Thurber

"Dogs are indeed the most social, affectionate, and amiable animals of the whole brute creation."


Edmund Burke

"Don't ever try to follow a dog act."



W.C. Fields

"Children and dogs are as necessary to the welfare of the country as Wall Street and the railroads."

Harry S. Truman

"They are better than human beings, because they know but do not tell."

Emily Dickinson

# About The Author

STEVE MATHIS is a pet owner and pet lover. A resident of Laguna Beach, California, he earned a masters degree in Education and is a former teacher and counselor. He is currently a sales manager for a leading real estate company in Orange County, California.

"Building balanced and equitable relationships is the key to successful living."